Review and Analysis of:

DRIVE:

THE SURPRISING TRUTH ABOUT WHAT MOTIVATES US

Daniel Pink

Summary Shorts

Book title: Review and Analysis of: Drive: The Surprising Truth About What Motivates Us By Daniel Pink.

–1st ed

ISBN: 978-0692741788

Printed in the United States of America

Book Cover Design: 'Summary Shorts' – Summary Media Inc

Introduction

So, what truly motivates us? Daniel Pink, in his remarkable book, 'Drive: The Surprising Truth About What Motivates Us' takes us on a journey to discover just that. In this review, we will Discuss and Analyze some of key concepts of the book. We will discover three main types of motivation, Motivation 1.0 and Motivation 2.0, the latter of which still motivates us today. He later goes on to say that there is a better way, a Motivation 3.0. a motivation based upon the inner sense of fulfillment. Let us explore 'Drive: The Surprising Truth About What Motivates Us' and learn what exactly these three types of Motivation are and how they stack up next to one another.

Concept Summary

Concept # 1: Our Basic Needs and Reward and Punishment.

Concept # 2: Motivation 3.0 - Intrinsic Vs Extrinsic Incentives.

Concept # 3: The Reward and Punishment Paradigm is No longer Needed.

Concept # 4: Exterior Incentives is Negatively Correlated To Motivation.

Concept # 5: The Path to Passion is The Drive To Excel.

Concept # 6: A Sense of Meaning Means Everything.

Concept # 7: Intrinsic Motivation Is Positively Correlated with Self Determination.

Concept # 8: Implementing Motivation 3.0.

Concept # 1: Our Basic Needs and Reward and Punishment

Our ancient, pre-historic Forbearers were concerned with pretty much one thing, survival. A place to hide from the elements and from predators, reproduction, food and drink. All things we today take for granted. This ancient preoccupation Daniel Pink calls Motivation 1.0. Humanity has lived with this type of motivation until just a few centuries ago.

Now things are vastly different. Starting around the time of the industrial revolution, things became a bit more complicated and complex. A new kind of motivation emerged. Motivation 2.0, this kind of motivation is fueled by the extrinsic. Mainly reward and punishment. You were rewarded for good performance and punished for bad. These types of rewards either rewarded good behavior or punished bad ones. That is pretty much what you will find in most business and school environments today.

As a result of Motivation 2.0, most employees do not feel fulfilled by their work; trying to avoid anything that would burden them with more responsibility. If only one employee would do this that is bad enough, but almost all the other employees are thinking

and doing the same thing. This created the need for enforcement

by management. This management style persists until this day.

Professor Harry Harlow changed the way we looked upon motivation and what makes us tick. At first that was not his intention, but the results of his experimentation shattered the motivation 2.0 paradigm. In his experiment, he gave eight Rhesus monkeys a mechanical puzzle to solve. In this experiment, if the monkeys solved the puzzle he would neither reward nor punish them. He figured without this reward or fear of punishment the monkeys would not be interested in the puzzle.

What he found however, changed everything. The monkeys actually figured out the puzzle and with great enthusiasm solved the puzzle and it was apparent they were very happy to have solved it. This was interesting because they were not give any incentive to solve the puzzle. Turns out the monkeys display a very similar behavior as we do.

Daniel Pink used Wikipedia as an example of people doing something for the sheer enjoyment of doing something. Wikipedia is managed mostly by people who write and edit the entries on their own free time, all volunteers. They don't get paid anything. It is the sheer pleasure of doing this kind of work that is its own reward. He is on to something. He goes on to use a similar product, Encarta created by Microsoft to prove his case. Encarta only used high paid content authors and editors to create content and yet, they closed down. This is a perfect example of Motivation 3.0 at play.

This shows that what motivated the monkeys and the Wikipedia writers is intrinsic motivation. They decided when and how to work on a project, it was not dictated by pay or any external reward.

Concept # 3: The Reward and Punishment Paradigm is

No longer Needed.

The reward and punishment paradigm has several unforeseen

consequences. Daniel Pink gives the example of Auto mechanics.

Many are given an incentive to perform X amount of repairs every

month in order to get a reward. It was discovered that the

mechanic didn't care if the customer was satisfied or not, all they

cared about was the rewards. This is not surprising since the

"crooked mechanic" is a cliché at this point. So, in this case the

whole system malfunctions; it doesn't promote efficiency in the

work process but the exact opposite since the mechanics would

make many unnecessary repairs.

Another example Daniel Pink uses is a study on agility that was

performed in India. The test subjects were promised money if

they were able to hit certain targets with a tennis ball. The ones

promised the money performed very poorly. It was discovered

that the reward put pressure on the subjects to perform well on

the task.

Before we continue I would like to say that motivation 2.0 is not

all bad. For routine tasks, it is very effective, but for endeavors and jobs that require higher level knowledge and creativity,

Motivation 2.0 can be very harmful on performance and even lead

to immoral acts.

Concept # 4: Exterior Incentives is Negatively Correlated To Motivation.

Children by nature are intrinsically motivated, if you see them play, they play for the joy of playing. It's fun and the experience is what drives their motivation. In other words, it is intrinsic. As they age the novelty wears of and the paradigm shifts to motivation 2.0 where their actions are no longer done for the sake of the action but because they will either be rewarded or punished for them. Daniel Pink used as an example a Nursery experiment. They asked children to draw. Some of the children were offered a certificate once completed and others were not offered anything as a reward. In the next experiment, this time neither side was offered a reward. It was found that the children who got the certificate during the first experiment no longer wanted to draw the second time around without a reward. The ones who did not get a certificate the first time didn't mind drawing again for no reward.

It was concluded that the first experiment extinguished the intrinsic motivation of the children who were given the reward. As it is called the "IF-THEN" rewards were proven detrimental. This has happened to most of us adults as well. We have lost much of our intrinsic reward capabilities because of our indoctrination into

the Motivation 2.0 paradigm.

We have heard it said that the "flow" state is the ideal state to be in order to excel. It turns out, that is very true. People of any profession who truly love it want to produce more and more of the thing they love. Photographers want to take more photos; a musician wants to create more music and writers want to produce more writings etc. They all use intrinsic motivation to spur them on because they are passionate about what they do.

In the book, Daniel Pink indicated that 50% of employees in the United States have and feel little to no commitment to their jobs. This is understandable because the jobs don't offer any true meaning to their lives and there are fewer opportunities to truly grow and express their personal interests and passions.

Those who have a passion for what they do almost always enter the state of "flow" which is simply a state of very concentrated focus and passion. It's for this reason they experience time just "flying by". Have you ever experienced that? If so, you have experienced flow as well. It may not last long, flow usually is episodic, but it's during those moments when the most gets done.

If employers would give jobs to workers that would encourage the

person to grow and improve, they too will get into the flow state

and this will increase productivity on the job and it will have an

added benefit of boosting morale.

The key is to work with passion.

One of the things many people lack is a sense of purpose and meaning.

An experiment was conducted in which several graduate students of the University of Rochester were asked about what they thought was their meaning in life. While many mentioned money and other motivation 2.0 based items; others mentioned they wanted to better themselves and others, clearly intrinsic Motivation 3.0 based items.

A few years later the researcher caught up to these students and wanted to see how their lives turned out. The ones with Motivation 2.0 goals did not find any more happiness in achieving what they set out to achieve. In fact, many suffered from anxiety and depression. The ones with Motivation 3.0 goals turned out to be much happier and lead relatively good lives with few incidences of mental health disturbances.

What was gleaned from this was that motivation 3.0 goals are far more conducive to happiness and the development of personal strength and resilience. Several studies since have been conducted with the same results.

A Sense of Meaning, Means Everything.

Some of the newer tech companies such as Google have a very positive work environment. They allow their employees to work naturally and via the motivation 3.0 paradigm. Part of why this works for them is because they allow their employees to take up to 20% of their time to develop their own ideas. Anyone can see that Googles approach is clearly a success.

Daniel Pink Also mentions the company Meddius. They don't have set working hours, all they require is that an employee finish their assigned task within a set period of time. How they chose to spend their time is up to them so long as they make the deadline. This allows for much flexibility and the employees have proven that this is an efficient way to work. In short, the employees have a sense of self determination.

Another great example cited is Zappos. Zappos has many people to take orders and provide customer service. Most call center type jobs have a very high, 35% turnover rate. Zappos is different. They allow employees to work from home and do not need to adhere to any pre-written script, they can be themselves with the customers. This leads to a very low turnover rate AND higher

motivation. It is no surprise they are also the leader in exceptional

customer service.

Despite the copious amounts of proof that Motivation 3.0 is far more effective than any other known system, most companies do not implement it. Most are still stuck in the old Motivation 2.0 paradigm.

It's been proven when you give an employee room to grow and to be self-determined they will perform better and with great passion and effort. In order to implement this, employees should have their work oriented towards more communal endeavors and have their work perhaps tied to programs that include social involvement. When they work, they are knowing that they are contributing to something bigger than themselves. A company that has the foresight to do this will find that they will not only be more profitable, but they will have happier, self-determined employees that will go the extra mile for them.

It is time to embrace. Motivation 3.0

Summary

To understand what motivates us, we must understand what motivation is and what forms of motivation we can use in our lives and organizations. By sticking to the old Motivation 2.0, we are creating an environment that demotivates people. Over time, the employees no longer produce their best work and begin to erode the effectiveness of the company. To remedy this, we must embrace Motivation 3.0 and allow people to be self-determined and this will allow them to enter the flow so they can grow and in turn improve the company's bottom line.

Drive, By Daniel Pink is a lucid and clear read. There are moments when it gets a bit dense with information about studies, but overall, it has a gripping narrative that makes you want to turn the page. The science behind the claims are rock solid and verifiable. It is certainly one of the best books on the topic of motivation.

Please see original book at Amazon.com.

ABOUT SUMMARY SHORTS

We at Summary Shorts understand that you are busy. We also know that you want to learn but simply don't have the time to read an entire book. We understand. It is our goal to give you the most concise review of books without sacrificing quality. Other review services tend to be light on information. We don't make that mistake. Summary Shorts Publications are available in several formats for your convenience. We are also going to offer other interesting and educational services on our site, including SHORT FACTS, a short video series teaching random facts from the books we review. We are also offering mini courses on various topics. Please check out our Website at

www.summaryshorts.com

ABOUT SUMMARY MEDIA INC

Summary Media Inc, is a small publishing company specializing in History, Spirituality, Psychology and Health and countless other topics.

Founded by Doron Alon, a pioneer in the self-publishing industry, and a bestselling author with well over 90 titles spanning several genres.

Review and Analysis of Mohamed A. El-Erian The Only Game in Town: Central Banks, Instability, and Avoiding the Next Collapse

Review and Analysis of: Aja Raden's: Stoned: Jewelry, Obsession, and How Desire Shapes the World

Review and Analysis of: Alan Watts's: The Wisdom of Insecurity: A Message for an Age of Anxiety

Review and Analysis of: Alex Cuadros's: Brazillionaires: Wealth, Power, Decadence, and Hope in an American Country

Review and Analysis of: Ayaan Hirsi Ali's: Heretic: Why Islam Needs A Reformation Now

Review and Analysis of: Benny Lewis's: Fluent in 3 Months: How Anyone at Any Age Can Learn To Speak Any Language From Anywhere in the World

Review and Analysis of: Carl Zimmer's: A Planet Of Viruses

Review and Analysis of: Dan Ariely's: Payoff: The Hidden Logic That Shapes Our Motivations

Review and Analysis of: Danielle LaPorte's: The Desire Map: A Guide to Creating Goals With Soul

Review and Analysis of: Marcus Aurelius's: Meditations

Review and Analysis of: Meltdown: A Free-Market Look at Why the Stock Market Collapsed, the Economy Tanked, and Government Bailouts Will Make Things Worse

Review and Analysis of: Pope Francis's: The Name of God Is Mercy

Review and Analysis of: The Bulletproof Diet: Lose up to a Pound a Day, Reclaim Energy and Focus, Upgrade Your Life

Review and Analysis of: The Ultimate Introduction to NLP: How to build a successful life

Review and Analysis of: Vishen Lakhiani's: The Code of the Extraordinary Mind: 10 Unconventional Laws to Redefine Your Life and Succeed On Your Own Terms

Review and Analysis of: Thomas M. Campbell II and T. Colin Campbell's: The China Study

FUTURE REVIEWS BY SUMMARY SHORTS

Review and And Analysis of: Cosmosapiens By John Hands

Review and And Analysis of: Freakonomics By Steven Levitt and Stephen Dubner

Review and And Analysis of: The Power of Habit By Charles Duhigg

Review and And Analysis of: Green Illusions By Ozzie Zehner

Review and And Analysis of: Emotional Intelligence By Daniel Goleman

Review and And Analysis of: Less Doing More Living By Ari Meisel

Review and And Analysis of: Micromotives and Macrobehaviors By Thomas Schelling

Review and And Analysis of: Six Thinking Hats by Edward de Bono

Review and And Analysis of: A Whole New Mind By Daniel Pink

Review and And Analysis of: Thinking Fast And Slow by Daniel Kahneman

Review and And Analysis of: Enchantment By Guy Kawasaki

Review and And Analysis of: Quiet By Susan Cain

Review and And Analysis of: The Wisdom of Psychopaths by Kevin Dutton

Review and And Analysis of: Predictably Irrational By Dan Ariely

Review and And Analysis of: Naked Economics by Charles Wheelan

Review and And Analysis of: Stumbling On Happiness By Daniel Gilbert

Review and And Analysis of: Mindset by Carol Dweck

Review and And Analysis of: Getting Things Done by David Allen

Review and And Analysis of: Flashboys by Michael Lewis

Review and And Analysis of: Crippled America by Donald Trump

Review and And Analysis of: Comfortably Unaware By Richard A. Oppenlander

Review and And Analysis of: Me, Myself And Us by Brian R. Little

Review and And Analysis of: Mindset by Carol Dweck

Review and And Analysis of: The Miracle Morning by Hal Elrod

And Many More. Please visit

WWW.SUMMARYSHORTS.COM to find out more.

9 781976 428470